the **complete** *series*

Soups

WILEY

John Wiley & Sons, Inc.

For general information on our other products and services or for technical support,
please contact our Customer Care Department within the United States at (800) 762-2974,
outside the United States at (317) 572-3993 or fax (317) 572-4002.

Wiley also publishes its books in a variety of electronic formats. Some content that
appears in print may not be available in electronic books. For more information about
Wiley products, visit our web site at www.wiley.com.

Library of Congress Cataloging-in-Publication Data is available upon request.

ISBN 978-1-118-11979-2

Printed in China

10 9 8 7 6 5 4 3 2 1

Contents

Introduction

Soup is one of the most basic foods. Its history stretches far into the past when soup was simply water simmered with whatever basic ingredients were available for flavor. Soup then was never about quality ingredients and complex flavors. Rather, it was simply about survival. Yet soup was still a meal shared between family members and acquaintances.

Thick hearty soups are served in the cold months to nourish and satisfy hungry children and to give energy to people at the end of a hectic day.

Cold refreshing soups are served in hot weather and humid climates to invigorate and enliven after an exhausting day.

Throughout the Western world soups are served as a teaser to the coming meal, while in China soup is served after a meal as an invigorating finale. In many European countries soup is served between courses to refresh the palate.

In fact, soup is served more often and in many more flavor combinations throughout the world than any other meal.

Soups have changed in many ways over the years, with modern cooking methods and ingredients taking over from traditional methods and ingredients.

What would Great Grandpa have said if Great Grandma had served him up a soup of onions cooked in white wine and brandy? The very idea! Soups made from rock melon and peaches. Soups with Japanese liqueur in them. Soups served chilled!

Ah yes times have changed.

It could be argued that the level of a nation's culinary sophistication can be seen in the soups it serves. There's nothing wrong with good old traditionals like beef shin or calf's foot, however we tend now to use more modern ingredients.

The modern cook prefers to stay away from the predictable and concentrate on a selection of recipes that use imaginative ingredients in imaginative ways. In the recipe selection offered in these chapters we include, with the traditional, some delightful variations.

When planning your dinner party, choose your soup carefully. A dinner of several courses should be preceded by a light clear soup, preferably a consommé. Thick soups, on the other hand, should be regarded as part of the main meal. And, of course, fruit soups may be served before or after the meal.

Soups are time-honored comfort foods, with well-rounded flavors and soothing, sustained warmth. Prepared more often in a single pot, they can incorporate all kinds of ingredients in combinations that are as nutritious as they are delicious.

Be lost in a sense of well-being as the contents of your cooking pot boil and bubble and the tendrils of steam and aroma curl up, permeating the surroundings and inducing a real warmth and homely feeling. What dreary winter afternoon is not brightened by the companionable murmur of a simmering soup on the stove?

A soup can be thick or thin, it can range from a clear, light broth to a hearty chowder almost thick enough to eat with a knife and fork. It has been noted that several centuries ago soup was served over 5 courses as a total meal. This has not been repeated in these modern times to our knowledge.

At the turn of the century it was normal to have soup always be served as part of the evening meal. These days however, we are not as regimented and soup can be served at any time of the night or day and in almost any position on the menu – from snack to main course, from entrée to dessert. Or indeed, soups can and sometimes do constitute an entire meal.

So you will see in these recipes that a soup can be served as a first course, a main course, or even – when made with fruit – a dessert. It can also be a between-meal snack, to satisfy those cheeky customers just home from school or work.

Our selected recipes offer soups of all types for all occasions and are built upon one of the basic stock recipes that appear in this introduction. Most are simple to prepare and in most situations require a minimum investment in time.

Of course, we offer slow-cooked soups as well as some real fast heat and serve varieties, a selection of recipes to suit all appetites and tastes.

Techniques

While soup is very easy to make and delightfully satisfying to eat, there is no doubt that a few tricks of the trade and some handy hints will give you superior results, even if you have never made a pot of soup before.

Cookware

While quality cookware is always a joy to use, remember that soups are centuries old and most of our ancestors didn't have the pleasure of shiny new cookware and elegant stovetops. Just use whatever large saucepans or stockpots you have. If you find you need a new saucepan, purchase a high-quality pot with a strong enamel or non-stick surface, or a stainless steel pot that has an insulated base. Cast iron works well too.

Ingredients

We all want to use the best, freshest ingredients when we prepare foods for our family or friends, and there is no doubt that quality ingredients contribute towards a more delicious and healthy end result. Meat, fish, poultry, spices and herbs should always be in peak condition for the best soups. Vegetables, however, can be a little wilted or past their prime. When you are about to make a soup or stock, clean out your vegetable crisper and see what has been left behind. Of course, common-sense should prevail, so don't use any vegetables that smell unpleasant or are obviously mouldy.

Most soups freeze well. When freezing any liquid, leave a 5mm space between the soup and the lid of the container, as liquid expands during freezing.

Home-made stocks – foundations of flavor

The basis of a quality soup is a quality stock – it's as simple as that! In years past, a good soup always began with hours of simmering simple vegetables and, perhaps, some meat bones to create a rich broth.

These days, however, if you prefer to bypass this step, there are several prepared stocks available from your local supermarket. They can be found in liquid form, as a paste or as a powder.

Generally speaking, it is much easier to purchase liquid stocks as they have a true flavor and are literally ready to use. Pastes are a good option too because they are concentrated, which allows you to add as much water as necessary to dilute the flavor according to your tastes.

In our opinion, most stock powders should be avoided if the liquid or paste stocks are available. These powders are often heavily salted and therefore offer a salty rather than 'true to taste' flavor. The ratio of powder to water can be difficult to master and some brands contain artificial flavors and colors.

By far the most rewarding and delicious stock is the one you make yourself. Contrary to popular belief, stocks are not difficult to make and, although they do need to simmer for quite some time, their preparation time is minimal.

The following recipes will guide you through the basics of making a good stock – regardless of which type of stock you wish to make, you can follow one of these basic methods. If you have any vegetables in your refrigerator that are looking a little wilted and sad, throw these into the stockpot too as they will add extra flavor and color.

Oh, and one other thing – remember that stocks freeze extremely well for extended periods of time, so don't be afraid to make a pot of stock when you have large amounts of vegetables, roasted meat bones or turkey frames (from the Christmas bird) on hand. Make the stock and pop it in the freezer for your future risotto or soup.

Making good stock is a very simple procedure. The ingredients are simmered in a pot – when strained and degreased the cooking liquid becomes a savoury extract to serve on its own, store for later use, or use in preparing another dish. Recipes for the five basic stocks follow on the next pages. Stock comes from humble beginnings – inexpensive cuts of meat and bones, fish bones and heads, or chicken wings and backs.

Attention to detail will reward you with a rich and tasty stock. All large fat deposits should be removed beforehand, but large bones will give you treasured gelatine, if cracked first, and provide body to your stock.

During cooking, remove scum that occasionally collects on top of the liquid. Scum consist of protein particles released by meat and bones, these float to the surface, where they gather in a foam. As nutritious as it is, the foam must be removed lest it cloud the stock. Skim off the foam as it forms at the start of cooking, skim thereafter only as the recipe directs.

After its initial rapid cooking, stock must not be allowed to return to rapid boil as the turbulence will muddy the liquid. As a final cleansing, the stock should be strained through a fine sieve or a colander lined with muslin.

Storage

To prepare stock for storage, divide it among containers surrounded with iced water. Wait until the stock has cooled to cover the containers, otherwise it may sour. Refrigerated in covered containers, any of these stocks will keep up to three days. The fat on top of the stock will form a temporary seal, helping to keep it fresh – you need not degrease the stock until shortly before you are ready to use it.

To prolong the life of refrigerated stock, first remove and discard the congealed fat, then boil the stock for five minutes – either freeze the stock or boil it again every three days. As always, cool it quickly and uncovered before storing it once more.

Fish and vegetable stock may be frozen for two months. Stock destined for the freezer must first be degreased, as frozen fat can turn rancid.

One Final Note

You will notice that the recipes in this book usually serve 4–8 or more people. This is because soup generally keeps very well and is often even better on the second or third day. Therefore, one recipe can offer you sustenance and an easy nutritional choice for several meals. If you prefer not to make such a large serve, or if you are cooking for only one or two people, most of these recipes can be halved successfully.

Rich Vegetable Stock

Suggested Ingredients
2 tablespoons olive oil
1 turnip or parsnip
5 cloves garlic
3 stalks celery
3 large carrots
10 mushrooms
3 large onions
4 tomatoes
2 leeks, well washed
2 parsnips
10 sprigs parsley
1 teaspoon peppercorns
4 bay leaves

1 Wash all the vegetables and chop roughly.
2 Heat the olive oil in a large stockpot and sauté all the vegetables for 20 minutes until they begin to develop a golden color on the surface.
3 Add the parsley, peppercorns, bay leaves and water to cover (about 4 quarts/liters) and bring to a boil. Simmer for 3 hours, skimming the surface to remove any scum that accumulates.
4 Add salt if desired, then simmer for an additional few minutes if you would like a more intense flavor. Allow to cool then strain, pressing on the solids. Use within three days or freeze for up to 12 months.

These are some suggested vegetables for a rich stock, but you can use whatever you have on hand. Even vegetables that are past their prime work just fine—Brussels sprouts, bell peppers, even corn.

Makes 8 cups • Preparation 25 minutes • Cooking 2 hours

Chicken Stock

Suggested Ingredients
2 carrots
4 stalks celery
3 onions
1 leek, chopped
8 sprigs parsley, chopped
2kg/4 lb chicken frames or wings
1 teaspoon peppercorns

1 Wash all the vegetables and chop roughly.
2 Place all ingredients in a large stockpot. Add water to generously cover the
   ingredients (about 4 quarts/liters). Bring to a boil then simmer for 2–3 hours,
   skimming the scum off the surface as it rises to the top.
3 Add salt if desired, then strain the stock through a sieve lined with cheesecloth.
4 Place in a large saucepan and chill until the fat solidifies on the surface. Remove
   the fat and use or freeze.

Makes 10 cups • Preparation 20 minutes • Cooking 3 hours

Fish Stock

Suggested Ingredients
500g/1 lb fish bones, heads and trimmings, washed
2 carrots, chopped
4 stalks celery, chopped
3 onions, roughly chopped
8 sprigs parsley, chopped
6 white peppercorns
good pinch of ground nutmeg
1 teaspoon salt

1 Place the fish pieces and 4 cups water into a saucepan and bring to a boil.
2 Skim off any discolored froth from the top. Add remaining ingredients and simmer gently, uncovered, for an additional 30 minutes. If cooked too long the stock becomes bitter.
3 Strain and discard the bones and vegetables. Use the stock within two days or freeze it in a sealed container.

Makes 4 cups • Preparation 30 minutes • Cooking 40 minutes

Shrimp Stock

Suggested Ingredients
1kg/2 lb shrimp shells and heads
2 carrots
4 stalks celery
3 onions
1 leek
8 sprigs parsley, chopped
1 teaspoon peppercorns

1 Thoroughly wash shells and heads.
2 Wash all the vegetables and chop roughly. Place in a large stockpot with the shrimp shells, heads, parsley and peppercorns. Cover with 4 quarts/ liters cold water and bring to a boil. Reduce heat to simmer and cook for 1–2 hours, skimming the skum off the surface as it forms.
3 Add salt to taste, then strain through a sieve lined with cheesecloth.
4 Place in a large saucepan and chill until the fat solidifies on the surface. Remove the fat and use or freeze the stock.

Makes 4 cups • Preparation 35 minutes • Cooking 2 hours

Veal Stock

Suggested Ingredients
1kg/2 lb veal breast or shin, cut into 3 in/75mm pieces
2kg/4 lb veal bones, cracked (preferably knuckles)
2 carrots
4 stalks celery
3 onions
4 sprigs fresh thyme, leaves removed and stalks discarded
3 unpeeled cloves garlic, crushed
8 black peppercorns
1 bay leaf

1 Rinse veal bones with water.
2 Wash all the vegetables and chop roughly. Place in a large stockpot with the veal bones, meat and remaining ingredients.
3 Wash all the vegetables and slice or chop roughly. Then place in a large stockpot with the veal bones and meat and all remaining ingredients.
4 Cover with cold water (about 4 quarts/liters), bring to a boil and simmer for 2–3 hours, skimming the scum off the surface as it rises to the top.
5 Add salt if desired, then strain through a sieve lined with cheesecloth.
6 Place in a large saucepan and chill until the fat solidifies on the surface. Remove the fat and use or freeze the stock.

Makes 10 cups • Preparation 30 minutes • Cooking 4 hours

Beef Stock

Suggested Ingredients
1kg/2 lb beef, cut into 3 in/75mm pieces
2kg/4 lb beef bones, cracked
2 carrots, chopped
4 stalks celery, chopped
3 onions, chopped
3 unpeeled cloves garlic, crushed
8 black peppercorns
3 cloves
4 sprigs fresh thyme, leaves removed and stalks discarded
1 bay leaf

1 Preheat oven to 220°C, place meat, bones, carrots, celery and onions in a large roasting pan and roast for about 1 hour, until well browned.
2 Transfer the contents of the roasting pan to a large saucepan. Pour 2 cups of water into the roasting pan and, with a spatula, scrape up all the brown bits from the bottom and sides of the pan. Pour this liquid into the large saucepan.
3 Add the garlic, peppercorns and cloves. Pour in enough water to cover the contents of the saucepan by about 3 in/75mm. Bring to a boil, then reduce heat to a simmer and skim off any impurities from the surface. Add the thyme and bay leaf, then simmer the stock for about 4 hours, skimming occasionally.
4 When cooked, strain the stock, allow to cool and refrigerate until fat solidifies on the surface. Remove the fat and use or freeze the stock.

Makes 10 cups • Preparation 40 minutes • Cooking 5 hours

Beef

There is nothing like the delicious aroma of home-made soup wafting through your home. The only thing that comes close is the satisfaction you feel when you have made a sensational soup all by yourself! The only difficult thing about these recipes is deciding which one to cook first.

Vegetable Beef Soup

2kg/4 lb beef shanks
2 tablespoons olive oil
1 teaspoon salt
1 small onion, chopped
450g/16 oz canned diced tomatoes
6 sprigs parsley
5 carrots, sliced
100g/3½ oz green beans, cut diagonally
1 medium potato, diced
1 stalk celery, chopped
¼ cup barley

1 In a heavy-based frying pan, brown the meat in the olive oil. Pour off excess fat and oil.
2 Cover with 8 cups cold water and bring to a boil. Add salt and onion, simmer for 2 hours.
3 Add vegetables and barley. Simmer for about 1 hour longer. Remove meat from bone, add back to soup and serve.

Serves 8 • Preparation 30 minutes • Cooking 3 hours 15 minutes

Beef Barley Soup

⅓ cup wholewheat flour
1 teaspoon salt
500g/1 lb lean stewing beef
2 tablespoons olive oil
1 medium onion, chopped
4 large cloves garlic, minced
½ medium carrot, grated
1 stalk celery, chopped
1 large tomato, diced
1 cup barley
5 cups chicken stock
¼ cup basil, chopped
1 bay leaf
salt and freshly ground black pepper

1 In a plastic bag, combine flour, salt and meat. Shake vigorously.
2 In a large saucepan, pour in the oil and quickly brown the meat over medium heat. Add onions and garlic and cook until soft, about 3–4 minutes. Add the carrot, celery and tomato and continue cooking for about 5 minutes.
3 Add barley, stock and basil and bring to a boil. Wrap the bay leaf in cheesecloth and add to the pot. Lower heat and allow to simmer until the barley is soft, about 20–25 minutes.
4 Season to taste with the salt and pepper. Remove bay leaf before serving.

Serves 8 • Preparation 20 minutes • Cooking 30 minutes

Hungarian Goulash Soup

3 tablespoons olive oil
2 medium white onions, sliced
2 tablespoons Hungarian (mild) paprika
2 cloves garlic, minced
2 teaspoons caraway seeds
8 sprigs fresh marjoram, leaves removed
and stalks discarded
500g/1 lb diced beef
400g/14 oz canned diced tomatoes
2 tablespoons tomato paste
6 cups beef stock
2 teaspoons brown sugar

1 teaspoon salt
1 teaspoon pepper
400g/14 oz potatoes, diced
200g/7 oz carrots, diced
1 tablespoon cornstarch, mixed with
2 tablespoons cold water
¼ cup sour cream
2 dill pickles, finely diced

1 Heat the olive oil in a saucepan and sauté the onion until golden brown, about
  5 minutes. Add the paprika, garlic, caraway seeds and marjoram and cook for
  1–2 minutes until the mixture is fragrant.

2 Add the beef, diced tomatoes and tomato paste, and cook until the meat is well
  coated and is a rich brown color, about 5 minutes. Add the stock, sugar, salt
  and pepper and bring to a boil. Simmer for 1 hour. Add the potatoes, carrots
  and continue cooking for an additional 30 minutes.

3 Check seasonings and adjust if necessary. Stir the cornstarch mixture into the
  soup, mixing well. Allow the soup to thicken for a couple of minutes, then serve
  in individual bowls.

4 Garnish with sour cream and pickles.

Serves 8 • Preparation 30 minutes • Cooking 1 hour 45 minutes

Meatball Soup

500g/1 lb ground beef
1 medium onion, finely chopped
¼ cup parsley, chopped
¼ cup medium-grain rice
2 eggs
salt and freshly ground black pepper
⅓ cup cornstarch
4 cups beef stock
50g/3½ tablespoons butter
⅓ cup lemon juice

1 Combine the mince, onion, parsley, rice and 1 egg in a bowl, and mix well with your hands. Season well with salt and pepper. Using one tablespoon of mixture for each meatball, shape mixture into balls. Roll in cornstarch, shaking off any excess.

2 Bring the stock and the butter to a boil, then reduce the heat and place the meatballs in the stock. Cover and simmer for 45 minutes. Allow to cool slightly.

3 Whisk the remaining egg and lemon juice together in a bowl, then add ½ cup of warm stock. Pour this mixture back into the saucepan and heat very gently. Season with salt and pepper before serving.

Serves 4 • Preparation 20 minutes • Cooking 1 hour 10 minutes

Russian Cabbage Soup

30g/2 tablespoons butter
250g/9 oz beef, diced
125g/4½ oz chopped bacon
300g/10 oz cabbage, finely shredded
2 large tomatoes, peeled and diced
2 onions, diced
1 bay leaf
salt and freshly ground black pepper
4 cups beef stock
⅓ cup sour cream
40g/1.4 oz Parmesan cheese, grated

1 Melt butter in a large saucepan and sauté beef and bacon over a medium heat until browned.
2 Add half the cabbage and all the remaining ingredients except sour cream and Parmesan. Cover, bring to a boil, and simmer for 1½ hours. Add remaining cabbage and cook for 10–15 minutes or until tender. Stir in cream, sprinkle with Parmesan cheese and serve.

Serves 6 • Preparation 15 minutes • Cooking 2 hours

Oxtail Soup

1 oxtail
1 tablespoon seasoned flour
2 tablespoons oil
6 cups beef stock
1 carrot, sliced
1 small turnip, sliced
1 onion, roughly chopped
2 stalks celery, chopped
2–3 bay leaves
salt
pinch of cayenne pepper
juice of 1 lemon
1 teaspoon Worcestershire sauce
3 tablespoons sherry or Madeira

1 Coat oxtail in seasoned flour. Heat oil over a medium heat, add oxtail and cook until brown. Add stock and simmer for 2 hours. Skim off the froth.
2 Place vegetables and bay leaves in the stock and cook for an additional 15–20 minutes.
3 Remove meat from bones, return the meat to soup and reheat. Season with salt and cayenne pepper. Stir in lemon juice and Worcestershire sauce. Just before serving, add sherry.

Serves 8 • Preparation 30 minutes • Cooking 2 hours 30 minutes

Hearty Beef Soup

100g/3½ oz chickpeas
100g/3½ oz dried split peas
3 tablespoons butter
3 tablespoons mild curry powder
3 tablespoons garam masala
3 tablespoons fresh minced ginger
3 cloves garlic, minced
4 large onions, diced
2 leeks, well washed and chopped

400g/14 oz ground beef
3 medium carrots, grated
2 stalks celery, finely sliced
1 small cauliflower, divided into florets
1 bunch fresh cilantro, chopped
8 cups chicken or beef stock
4 tablespoons yogurt
salt and pepper to taste

1 Place the chickpeas and split peas in a large bowl of water and soak for 30 minutes. Drain. Heat the butter in a large saucepan and add the curry powder, garam masala, ginger and garlic and sauté until the spices are fragrant, about 3 minutes. Add the onions and leeks and cook over a medium-high heat until the onions have softened and are beginning to turn golden, about 6 minutes.

2 Add the minced beef and cook in the spice and onion mixture, making sure that the meat is thoroughly cooked and fragrant before continuing.

3 Add the carrots, celery, cauliflower, half the chopped fresh cilantro, the stock and the chickpea mixture and bring to a boil. Simmer the soup for 1½ hours or until the chickpeas are tender, stirring often.

4 When almost ready to serve, stir through the yogurt and add salt and pepper to taste. Garnish with the remaining chopped fresh cilantro and serve.

Serves 8–10 • Preparation 30 minutes plus 10 minutes soaking • Cooking 2 hours

Chicken

They say that chicken soup is good for the soul. All throughout history we hear of chicken soup being a cure for failing health. We make no such claims, but offer some of the best chicken soup recipes we could find and devise. You will find some great offerings in the pages of this chapter.

Chicken Vegetable Soup with Cheese Sticks

2 boneless, skinless chicken breasts
4 cups chicken stock
1 tablespoon canola oil
2 leeks, washed and thinly sliced
2 carrots, diced
2 stalks celery, diced
3 cloves garlic, crushed
6 cups spinach, arugula or escarole
3 tablespoons basil pesto
freshly cracked black pepper

Cheese Sticks
1 sheet puff pastry, thawed
40g/1.4 oz Cheddar cheese, finely grated

1 Put the chicken in a pot, add just enough chicken stock to cover it and poach gently for about 10 minutes or until just cooked. Set aside to cool.

2 Heat the oil in a large pot, add the leeks and cook gently for about 2 minutes until soft. Add the carrot, celery and garlic, strain the chicken poaching stock through a fine sieve and add to the vegetables with the rest of the stock. Simmer for 10 minutes. Chop the greens finely, add them to the soup and cook for an additional 10 minutes.

3 Shred the chicken breasts and add them to the soup. Stir in the pesto and season with plenty of cracked black pepper.

Cheese Sticks

1 Preheat the oven to 425°F/220°C. Cut the puff pastry into 1 in/2cm strips and place on a baking sheet lined with parchment paper. Sprinkle with the cheese and bake for 20 minutes or until crisp and golden.

2 Serve the soup in wide bowls with cheese sticks.

Serves 6 • Preparation 30 minutes • Cooking 40 minutes

Chicken and Corn Soup

1kg/2 lb chicken
½ cup water chestnuts, drained
1 small onion, peeled and halved
2 slices bacon, cooked and crumbled
½ in/1cm piece green ginger, peeled
450g/16 oz canned corn, drained reserving liquid
6 green onions, sliced
2 teaspoons sesame oil
salt and freshly ground black pepper
3 tablespoons cornstarch
1 tablespoon sherry
2 teaspoons soy sauce
1 egg

1 Wash chicken and place into a large saucepan with 10 cups water. Bring to a boil and simmer approximately 40 minutes or until chicken is cooked. Remove chicken from pan, set aside to cool. Do not discard chicken stock. While chicken is cooking, prepare other ingredients.

2 Place water chestnuts, onion, bacon and ginger into food processor or blender bowl and process until finely chopped. Remove from bowl.

3 Purée corn niblets in food processor or blender.

4 Remove skin and bones from chicken. Place chicken into processor bowl and process until finely chopped.

5 Take 2 cups of chicken stock from pan and reserve for future use.

6 Add all prepared ingredients with reserved corn liquid to chicken stock.

7 Add green onions to saucepan with sesame oil, salt and pepper. Bring to boil. Mix cornstarch and ⅓ cup water to a smooth paste, add to soup and simmer, stirring, for 3 minutes. Add sherry and soy sauce. Lightly beat egg with a fork, add to soup and stir for 1 minute. Serve.

Serves 12 • Preparation 40 minutes • Cooking 1 hour 30 minutes

Chicken and Leek Soup

1kg/2 lb chicken pieces
1 onion, chopped
1 carrot, peeled and chopped
pinch saffron
1 stalk celery, chopped
2 leeks, finely sliced
30g/2 tablespoons butter
salt
cayenne pepper
½ cup heavy cream

1 In a large pot, place the chicken, onion, carrot, saffron and celery. Cover the ingredients with water and boil for 1 hour.
2 Remove from the heat and strain off the stock. Reserve the chicken.
3 Sauté the leeks in the butter until soft, add the chicken stock and, heat through. Season with salt and cayenne pepper. Add cream as desired and serve.

Serves 6 • Preparation 10 minutes • Cooking 1 hour 15 minutes

Mulligatawny

30g/2 tablespoons butter
1 small onion, finely diced
½ in/1cm piece ginger, grated
1 tablespoon curry powder
1 tablespoon all-purpose flour
1 tablespoon desiccated coconut
4 cups chicken stock
1 bouquet garni
1 tablespoon tomato paste
1 tablespoon mango chutney
½ small banana, sliced
150g/5 oz cooked chicken breast, diced
juice of ½ lemon
salt and freshly ground black pepper

1 Melt butter in a saucepan over medium heat. Add onion, ginger and curry powder and cook until onion is tender. Add the flour and coconut and cook for an additional 2 minutes. Add the stock, bouquet garni and tomato paste. Bring to a boil and simmer over low heat for 45 minutes.
2 Add the chutney, banana, chicken, lemon juice and seasonings. Heat through, remove bouquet garni and serve sprinkled with boiled rice.

Serves 4 • Preparation 20 minutes • Cooking 1 hour

Hot and Sour Chicken Soup

600g/1⅓ lb boneless, skinless chicken breasts, cut into ½ in/1cm strips
2 tablespoons peanut oil
4 cloves garlic, minced
2 French shallots, chopped
5 stems of cilantro, leaves included, chopped
30g/1 oz fresh ginger, bruised
3 small red Thai chilies, minced
3 stalks lemongrass, bruised
6 kaffir lime leaves, finely shredded
8 cups chicken or vegetable stock
3 tablespoons fish sauce
100g/3½ oz cellophane or glass noodles
6 green onions, diagonally sliced
juice of 1–2 limes
½ cup cilantro leaves

1 Brush the chicken strips with 1 tablespoon of peanut oil and grill or pan-fry until the chicken is golden brown and slightly charred, about 3 minutes each side.

2 Heat the remaining tablespoon of peanut oil in a large saucepan and add the garlic, shallots, cilantro leaves and stems, ginger, chilies, lemongrass and lime leaves and toss in the hot oil until fragrant, about 2 minutes. Add the stock and bring to a boil. Simmer for 10 minutes, then add the grilled chicken strips and simmer for an additional 10 minutes.

3 Add the fish sauce and noodles and simmer for an additional 2 minutes, or until the noodles are tender. Add the sliced green onions, lime juice and cilantro leaves, remove the lemongrass and serve very hot.

Serves 6 • Preparation 30 minutes • Cooking 30 minutes

Matzo Ball Soup

Soup
2 tablespoons vegetable oil
3 large onions, chopped
3 large carrots, chopped
4 stalks celery, chopped
2kg/4 lb chicken bones, wings, scraps
4 bay leaves
6 sprigs parsley
300g/10 oz piece of beef top rib

Matzoh Balls
2 tablespoons vegetable oil
1 large onion, finely diced
4 large eggs
¼ small bunch chives, chopped
1–1½ cups matzoh meal
salt and freshly ground black pepper

1 First, make the soup. Heat the oil in a very large saucepan and add the onions, carrots and celery and sauté in the oil until golden, about 10 minutes. Add the chicken, bay leaves, parsley, beef and 4 quarts/liters of water and bring to a boil. Simmer for 5 hours, skimming the scum off the surface as it becomes visible. After 5 hours, taste the soup and season to taste. Chill the soup overnight.

2 The next day, skim the fat off the surface of the soup then reheat until just warm. Strain the soup into a clean saucepan, discarding the solids.

3 To make the matzoh balls, heat the vegetable oil in a frying pan and add the finely chopped onions. Sauté until the onions are deep golden brown. Remove the pan from the heat and add the eggs, chives, matzoh meal and salt and pepper to taste and mix thoroughly. Allow the mixture to chill for 2 hours.

4 Bring a large pot of salted water to a boil and then shape the matzoh mixture into walnut-size balls and drop them into a boiling water. Simmer for approximately 30 minutes or until tender. Remove with a slotted spoon and set aside.

5 To serve, reheat the soup until scalding then add the matzoh balls to heat them through. Serve 1–2 matzoh balls per person with a bowl of broth and garnish with extra parsley.

Serves 10 • Preparation 40 minutes • Cooking 6 hours

Chinese Chicken Noodle Soup

150g/5 oz chicken breast, cut into chunks
250g/10 oz Chinese mung bean vermicelli
½ cup button mushrooms, sliced
salt
½ teaspoon black or white pepper
1 green onion, chopped

Stock
3 teaspoons fish sauce
1 onion, quartered
1½kg/3 lb pork bones
500g/1 lb chicken wings, bones and/or leftover meat scraps
500g/1 lb of 2 of the following: whole carrot, quartered cauliflower, whole green beans, quarter of a cabbage

1 Make stock by boiling all ingredients together with 8 cups water, then simmering for 1 hour. Strain reduced stock and discard the bones and vegetables.
2 Boil chicken chunks in stock for 15 minutes, skimming scum from the surface. Add vermicelli and mushrooms, and cook until vermicelli is done.
3 Season with salt and pepper and serve sprinkled with chopped green onion.

Serves 6 • Preparation 30 minutes • Cooking 1 hour 20 minutes

Spicy Chicken Soup

2 teaspoons peanut oil, extra
6 cups chicken stock
3 cups shredded cooked chicken
400g/14 oz canned corn, drained
2 tablespoons kecap manis*
1–2 teaspoons sambal oelek (chili garlic sauce)
2 cups shredded spinach, washed and drained
salt to taste

Paste
2 shallots, chopped
2 cloves garlic
2 hazelnuts
1 teaspoon dried shrimp paste
2 teaspoons peanut oil

1 Crush or pound paste ingredients in a mortar with pestle or in a small
  food processor.
2 Heat oil in a large saucepan. Add paste and cook for 1–2 minutes. Add
  stock, chicken, sweetcorn, kecap manis and sambal oelek. Bring to a boil
  and simmer over low heat for 5–10 minutes.
3 Add spinach and cook for 1–2 minutes. Season with salt.

***Kecap manis is a sweet soy sauce that is available at Asian markets. If you
can't find it, you can substitute one part molasses and two parts soy sauce.**

Serves 4 • Preparation 20 minutes • Cooking 15 minutes

Chicken and Coconut Soup

3 cups coconut milk
500g/1 lb chicken breasts, cut into ½ in/1cm strips
1½ in/4cm piece of fresh ginger, sliced
2 stalks lemongrass, cut into 1½ in/4cm pieces
1 fresh cilantro root, bruised
4 kaffir lime leaves, shredded
3 fresh red chilies, seeded and chopped
2 tablespoons fish sauce
2 tablespoons lemon juice
¼ cup fresh cilantro leaves

1 Place coconut milk and 2 cups water in a saucepan and bring to a boil over a medium heat. Add chicken, galangal or ginger, lemongrass, cilantro root and lime leaves and simmer for 6 minutes.
2 Stir in chilies, fish sauce and lemon juice. To serve, ladle into bowls and scatter with cilantro leaves.

This popular Thai soup is known as tom kha gai. When dining in the traditional Thai manner, soups are not served as a separate course but are eaten with the other dishes and rice.

Serves 6 • Preparation 15 minutes • Cooking 15 minutes

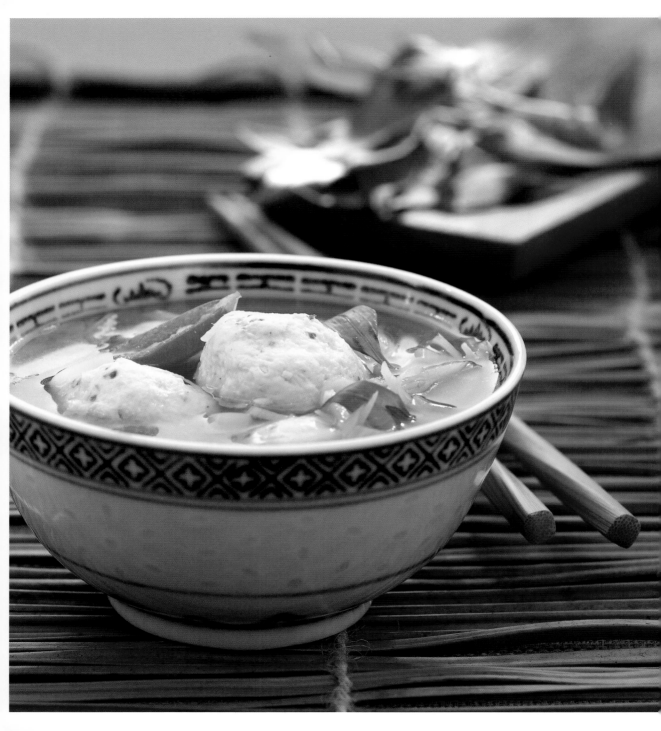

Chicken and Dumpling Soup

Dumplings
300g/10 oz chicken breasts, diced
1 egg white
50mL/3½ tablespoons cream
2 shallots, finely diced
1 clove garlic
2 small red chilies
1 tablespoon sesame oil
1 tablespoon fresh cilantro, chopped
1 teaspoon fish sauce
1 teaspoon salt
1 teaspoon white pepper

Chilli Broth
1½ quarts/liters chicken stock
3 small red chilies, seeded and cut lengthways
1 stem lemongrass, thinly sliced
20g/4 teaspoons ginger, thinly sliced
cilantro leaves, to garnish

1 In a food processor, combine all the dumpling ingredients and process until the mix is smooth and well blended.

2 Roll into walnut-sized balls.

3 To make the chilli broth, place the ingredients into a saucepan. Bring to a boil and reduce to a simmer for 10 minutes. Place half the dumplings into the simmering broth and cook for 5 minutes.

4 Remove cooked dumplings with a slotted spoon and keep warm. Cook the remaining dumplings. To serve, place dumplings into bowls and pour over the broth. Garnish with cilantro.

Serves 4–6 • Preparation 30 minutes • Cooking 20 minutes

Lamb

Soups that contain lamb cuts are both vivid and robust. This versatile meat can give some wonderful and unpredictable tastes when combined with a selection of vegetables, grains, herbs and spices. Our selections here vary from the traditional, yet offer great tastes and are easy to prepare.

Lamb Shank Soup

30g/2 tablespoons butter
1 large onion, sliced
4 lamb shanks
½ cup barley
3 stalks celery, sliced
2 large carrots, sliced
2 large parsnips, diced
2 tomatoes, diced
1 teaspoon salt
freshly ground black pepper
¼ cup parsley, chopped

1 Melt the butter in a large saucepan. Add the onion and cook over a low heat for 10 minutes. Add the shanks, barley, celery, carrots, parsnips, tomatoes and 12 cups water. Season with salt and pepper. Cover and simmer for 1½–2 hours.

2 Remove the lamb shanks and chop the meat. Return the meat to the soup and discard the bones. Adjust seasoning if necessary.

3 Sprinkle with parsley and serve with crusty bread.

Serves 8 • Preparation 30 minutes • Cooking 2 hours

Lamb and Cheddar Soup

750g/1.65 lb lamb neck bones
1 large onion, finely chopped
3 cloves garlic, finely chopped
2 bay leaves
30g/2 tablespoons butter
2 tablespoons all-purpose flour
1 cup milk
125g/4½ oz Cheddar cheese, grated
4 carrots, diced
2 leeks, finely chopped
3 medium potatoes, peeled and diced
salt and freshly ground black pepper
¼ cup fresh parsley, chopped

1 Place the lamb in a saucepan. Add the onion, garlic and bay leaves and cover with 4 cups water. Bring to a boil and simmer gently for an hour.

2 Remove the lamb and cut the meat into small pieces – discard the bones, but keep the lamb stock.

3 In a large saucepan, melt the butter and add the flour. Cook for a minute, stirring all the time, then add the milk.

4 Simmer the sauce for 2 minutes, add the cheese, the lamb stock, lamb pieces and vegetables. Simmer gently for 30 minutes, stirring occasionally. Season with salt and pepper to taste.

5 Serve garnished with chopped parsley and accompanied with crusty bread.

Serves 4 • Preparation 30 minutes • Cooking 1 hour 10 minutes

Smoky Lamb Soup

1kg/2 lb eggplant
80g/5½ tablespoons butter
2 large leeks
500g/18 oz sweet potato, peeled and cubed
2 teaspoons ground cumin
2 teaspoons ground cinnamon
2kg/4 lb lamb shanks
4 cups beef stock
4 sprigs thyme
3 cinnamon sticks
1 cup flat-leaf parsley, chopped

1 Preheat oven to 425°F/220°C. Prick eggplant all over and roast on an oiled baking sheet until browned and softened, about an hour. Chop the eggplant into bite-size pieces.

2 Heat half the butter in a large saucepan, add the leeks and sauté until golden. Add the chopped eggplant, sweet potato, cumin and ground cinnamon and stir thoroughly while cooking for 5 minutes or until all the ingredients are golden and fragrant. Place this mixture in a bowl and set aside.

3 In the same saucepan, heat the remaining butter and add the lamb shanks, and brown over medium-high heat. Add the beef stock, thyme, cinnamon sticks and 6 cups water and simmer for 1 hour.

4 Remove the shanks and, to the remaining soup, add the eggplant mixture and half the parsley. Simmer for 10 minutes. Cut all the meat off the lamb shanks and return this meat to the soup. Discard the bones.

5 Remove and discard the cinnamon sticks and thyme sprigs, then reheat the soup until simmering. Season to taste with salt and pepper. Add parsley.

Serves 6–8 • Preparation 1 hour • Cooking 2 hours

Lamb Chickpea Soup

1 tablespoon olive oil
1 large brown onion, finely chopped
500g/1 lb lamb stew meat, finely chopped
200g/7 oz canned chickpeas, rinsed and drained
3 tablespoons tomato purée
1 teaspoon ground coriander
1 teaspoon ground turmeric
½ teaspoon chilli powder
½ teaspoon salt
1½ tablespoons dried mint
juice of ½ lemon
6 fresh mint sprigs
1 lemon, cut into wedges

1 Heat the oil in a large casserole or saucepan. Gently fry the onion for a few minutes until pale golden and soft.

2 Add the lamb, chickpeas, tomato purée, spices and salt, cooking for a few more minutes and stirring well.

3 Add 4 cups water to the saucepan – this should cover the mixture – then add 1 cup more if required. If adding extra water, remember that you may need to add a little extra spice and salt to compensate.

4 Cover and simmer over a medium heat for approx 45–50 minutes or until the lamb is tender. If required, you may add a little extra water again at this point, but remember to adjust the seasoning if you do.

5 Add the dried mint and the lemon juice, return to the heat for an additional 3–4 minutes then serve each bowl with a sprig of fresh mint and a lemon wedge on the side.

Serves 6 • Preparation 20 minutes • Cooking 1 hour

Lamb and Barley Soup

4 lamb shanks, fat removed
6 cups beef stock
1 teaspoon salt
½ cup barley, washed
2 medium onions, finely diced
2 medium carrots, medium diced
2 stalks celery, thinly sliced
1 small turnip, medium diced
freshly ground black pepper
¼ cup parsley, chopped

1 Bring the lamb shanks, stock and salt to a boil. Add barley and bring back to a boil.
2 Skim off any froth from the surface, cover and gently simmer over low heat for 2–3 hours. Add vegetables and simmer for an additional 30 minutes.
3 Remove the shanks, chop the meat and add to the soup. Season with salt and pepper, garnish with parsley.

Serves 8 • Preparation 30 minutes • Cooking 3 hours 30 minutes

Pork

How about traditional pea soup or corn and bacon chowder? You will find some of your favorites in this chapter. You will also find many soups using pork cuts are offered in Asian restaurants with noodles, dumplings or wontons.

Broccoli Soup with Bacon

1 tablespoon olive oil
1 large onion, roughly chopped
2 cloves garlic, chopped
3 cups chicken stock
500g/1 lb broccoli
3 slices bacon, cooked and crumbled
1 cup milk
freshly ground black pepper

1 Heat the oil in a large saucepan and sauté the onion and garlic for 5 minutes until clear. Pour in stock and bring to a boil.

2 Add broccoli and cook for 10 minutes until just tender. Purée in a blender or food processor.

3 Return soup to saucepan. Mix in bacon and milk. Cook for 5 minutes. Season with freshly ground black pepper. Serve garnished with chopped chives.

Serves 4 • Preparation 15 minutes • Cooking 30 minutes

Asian Pork Soup

2 tablespoons olive oil
400g/14 oz pork tenderloin, cut into thin bite-size pieces
100g shiitake mushrooms, sliced
2 cloves garlic, minced
6 cups chicken stock
2 tablespoons dry sherry
2 tablespoons soy sauce
¾ in/2cm piece ginger, minced
¼ teaspoon red pepper
150g/5 oz Napa cabbage, thinly sliced
1 green onion, thinly sliced

1 Heat the oil in a large non-stick saucepan over medium heat. Add pork to hot saucepan and cook for 2–3 minutes or until slightly pink in center.
2 Remove from the saucepan and set aside. Add mushrooms and garlic to saucepan and stir until tender over medium heat.
3 Stir in chicken stock, sherry, soy sauce, ginger, and red pepper. Bring to a boil. Stir in pork, Chinese cabbage, and green onion, heat through and serve.

Serves 4 • Preparation 20 minutes • Cooking 20 minutes

Corn and Bacon Chowder

6 slices bacon, chopped
1 medium onion, thinly sliced
500g/1 lb potatoes, peeled and medium diced
880g/28 oz canned creamed corn
3 cups milk
1 sprig thyme, leaves removed and stalk discarded
salt and freshly ground black pepper
dash of Worcestershire sauce

1 Place bacon in a saucepan and sautè over medium heat until crisp. Remove and drain on absorbent paper.
2 Sautè onion until tender, add potatoes and 5 cups boiling water and cook for an additional 10 minutes. Add sweetcorn, milk, thyme and bacon, bring to a boil, season with salt, pepper and Worcestershire sauce. Garnish with extra fresh thyme or parsley.

Serves 8 • Preparation 30 minutes • Cooking 30 minutes

Egg Drop Soup

4 cups chicken stock
1½ tablespoons soy sauce
1 teaspoon sugar
2 eggs, lightly beaten
1 slice of ham, finely diced
2 green onions, finely chopped

1 Bring stock to a boil, and add soy sauce and sugar.
2 Just before serving, pour the eggs into the hot stock, but do not stir. As soon as the eggs start to cook, stir gently. Garnish with ham and green onions and serve immediately.

Serves 4 • Preparation 15 minutes • Cooking 15 minutes

Long Soup

¼ cup water chestnuts, drained
½ in/1cm piece ginger
125g/4½ oz bamboo shoots, drained
125g/4½ oz lean pork, cut into 1 in/25mm pieces
1 tablespoon oil
250g/9 oz cabbage, sliced
5 green onions, sliced
2 slices ham
12 cups chicken stock
salt and freshly ground black pepper
¼ cup soy sauce
90g/3 oz thin egg noodles
¼ cup sherry

1 Place ham, water chestnuts, ginger and bamboo shoots into food processor bowl.
   Process until finely chopped. Set aside.
2 Finely mince one-third of the cubed pork at a time. Heat oil in a large saucepan, add
   minced pork and cook for 5 minutes, stirring frequently. Add the cabbage, green
   onions, ham, water chestnuts, ginger, bamboo shoots, stock, salt, pepper, soy sauce
   and egg noodles. Bring to boil and simmer for 10 minutes or until noodles are tender.
   Stir in the sherry.

Serves 12 • Preparation 30 minutes • Cooking 30 minutes

Split Pea Soup

250g/9 oz dried split peas
500g/1 lb ham hocks or ham bones
2 carrots, roughly chopped
2 turnips, roughly chopped
2 onions, roughly chopped
4 stalks celery, chopped
salt and freshly ground black pepper
1 tablespoon all-purpose flour, mixed with 1 tablespoon water

1 Wash peas and soak in water overnight. Place peas, water and bones in a saucepan and bring to a boil. Add prepared vegetables and simmer for 1½ hours.
2 Remove bones, purée mixture, and season with salt and pepper. Thicken with flour paste and, stirring continuously, cook for 3 minutes. Garnish with croutons and serve immediately.

Serves 8 • Preparation 30 minutes • Cooking 2 hours

Pork and Vegetable Soup

400g/14 oz boneless pork, cut into ½ in/15mm cubes
2 tablespoons all-purpose flour
1 tablespoon vegetable oil
1 medium onion, chopped
2 stalks celery, diced
3 cups chicken stock
½ teaspoon dried marjoram
2 medium potatoes, peeled and diced
125g/4½ oz mushrooms, chopped
½ medium green bell pepper, chopped
2 tablespoons diced pimiento
¼ cup flat-leaf parsley, chopped

1 Place pork and flour in a plastic bag and shake until coated.

2 Heat oil in a large saucepan. Add the pork and brown lightly.

3 Add onion and sauté 2–3 minutes longer. Add celery, stock and marjoram. Bring to a boil. Cover and simmer for 15 minutes.

4 Add potatoes and mushrooms. Bring to a boil again. Cover and simmer for 10 minutes. Stir in green pepper and pimiento. Simmer for 5 minutes more.

5 Sprinkle with parsley. Ladle into bowls.

Serves 4 • Preparation 20 minutes • Cooking 45 minutes

Pork, Mushroom and Corn Soup

200g/7 oz lean pork
4 dried Chinese mushrooms
425g/15 oz canned baby corn
1 tablespoon oil
2 cloves garlic, crushed
½ teaspoon ground black pepper
1 cilantro plant, roots included, chopped
1 onion, chopped
2 tablespoons fish sauce
½ cup fresh basil, chopped

1 Chop pork and set aside. Soak dried mushrooms in boiling water for 30 minutes. Drain and slice. Drain baby corn and rinse well, then cut into bite-size pieces.
2 Heat oil in a large saucepan, add garlic, pepper, cilantro and onion and fry for 2 minutes. Add chopped pork and fry until pork is golden brown.
3 Add 4 cups water, fish sauce, baby corn and mushrooms and bring to a boil. Lower heat, cover and simmer for 10 minutes. Serve hot, sprinkled with chopped basil leaves.

Serves 4 • Preparation 30 minutes • Cooking 1 hour

Southwestern Pork Soup

1 tablespoon olive oil
1 medium onion, chopped
½ green bell pepper, chopped
4 large cloves garlic, minced
1 jalapeño pepper, seeded and minced
500g/1 lb pork tenderloin, trimmed and cut into bite-size pieces
2 cups chicken stock
2 teaspoons chilli powder
1 teaspoon ground cumin
½ teaspoon salt
¼ teaspoon black pepper
500g/18 oz canned pinto beans, rinsed and drained
400g/14 oz canned diced tomatoes, undrained
¼ cup fresh cilantro, chopped
1 avocado, diced

1 Heat a small non-stick casserole dish over medium-heat and add oil.

2 Add onion, bell pepper, garlic and jalapeño and sauté for 2 minutes.

3 Add pork and cook for 3 minutes. Add stock, chilli powder, cumin, salt, pepper, pinto beans and tomatoes and bring to a boil.

4 Partially cover, reduce heat, and simmer for 6 minutes or until pork is done, stirring occasionally. Remove from heat and stir in cilantro. Serve with avocado.

Serves 4 • Preparation 20 minutes • Cooking 15 minutes

Stone Soup

1 tablespoon olive oil
1 onion, finely chopped
2 cloves garlic, crushed
200g/7 oz smoked bacon, diced
250g/9 oz smoked ham hock
2 potatoes, diced
2 carrots, diced
2 turnips, diced
2 stalks celery, diced
2 bay leaves
6 cups vegetable or chicken stock
150g/5 oz Savoy or green cabbage, shredded
400g/14 oz canned red kidney beans, drained and rinsed
¼ cup fresh parsley, chopped
salt and freshly ground black pepper

1 Heat the oil in a large saucepan over medium heat. Cook the onion and garlic until soft. Add the bacon and cook for 2 minutes. Add the ham hock, potatoes, carrots, turnips, celery, bay leaves and stock.

2 Bring to a boil, reduce heat to low and simmer covered for 40–45 minutes or until vegetables are tender. If time permits, simmer for 1 hour, as this gives the soup more flavor. Add cabbage and kidney beans and simmer for an additional 5 minutes.

3 Remove ham hock and cut the meat into small pieces. Return meat to the saucepan, add parsley and season with salt and pepper. Serve with crusty bread.

Serves 4–6 • Preparation 25 minutes • Cooking 2 hours

Seafood

Somehow seafood always seems to be the perfect ingredient for a soup. The subtle, delicate flavor of fish combines perfectly with the fresh herbs and spices in these recipes. From shrimp to mussels, calamari to oysters, crabs to clams – these tempting choices are both delicious and deceptively simple to make.

Clam Chowder

45g/3 tablespoons butter
3 rashers bacon, chopped
1 onion, chopped
1 stalk celery, chopped
1 carrot, chopped
1 potato, peeled and chopped
280g/9–10 oz canned clams, drained and chopped
3 tablespoons all-purpose flour
2½ cups milk
salt and freshly ground black pepper
1 tablespoon brandy

1 Melt 1 tablespoon of butter in pan, add bacon and vegetables and cook gently until soft.
2 Add 1¼ cups water and potatoes to vegetables. Simmer until vegetables are tender, approximately 15–20 minutes.
3 Add clams to vegetables and remove the pan from the heat.
4 Melt remaining butter in pan, stir in the flour and cook for 1 minute. Remove from heat and gradually stir in milk.
5 Return soup to heat and add milk mixture. Cook until soup boils and thickens, stirring constantly. Season with salt and pepper, stir in the brandy and serve.

Serves 6 • Preparation 20 minutes • Cooking 30 minutes

Corn and Smoked Salmon Soup

300g/10 oz smoked salmon
8 cups fish stock
4 ears of corn
salt
cayenne pepper
4 egg yolks
1 cup heavy cream
8 sprigs of dill

1 Poach the smoked salmon in the fish stock for 5 minutes. You can add some white wine if desire.
2 Remove the salmon from the stock and cool. Cut the corn kernels from the cob. Place the kernels into the stock and boil until they are tender.
3 Blend or process the stock with the kernels. Return to the pot and season with salt and cayenne pepper. Flake the salmon, add to the soup and bring to a boil.
4 In a separate bowl, mix the egg yolks and the cream. Remove the soup from the heat and allow to cool a little. Add the egg yolks and cream, stirring constantly.
5 Heat until hot but not boiling, or the soup will curdle. Garnish with sprig of dill.

Serves 8 • Preparation 20 minutes • Cooking 40 minutes

Fish Stew

60g/4 tablespoons butter
1 small leek, washed and thinly sliced
1 medium carrot, thinly sliced
1 small onion, chopped
1 tablespoon curry powder
1 tomato, peeled, seeded and chopped
2 cups fish stock
1 large potato, peeled and diced
1 teaspoon brown sugar
½ teaspoon salt
250g/9 oz fish filets, cut into 1 in/25mm pieces
salt and freshly ground black pepper
1 cup heavy cream
¼ cup parsley, chopped

1 Heat butter in a saucepan and sauté leek, carrot and onion over a low heat for
   5 minutes or until the vegetables are tender.
2 Stir in curry powder and cook for 2 minutes. Add tomato and cook for 5 minutes.
   Stir in stock, potato, sugar and salt and bring to a boil. Reduce the heat and
   simmer for 15 minutes.
3 Add fish and seasonings and simmer for an additional 10 minutes. Stir through
   cream and reheat without boiling. Sprinkle with parsley and serve.

Serves 8 • Preparation 30 minutes • Cooking 45 minutes

Crab Corn Chowder

1 cup white wine
2 cloves garlic, crushed
4 cups good fish stock
1 teaspoon dried oregano
3 green onions, sliced
220g/8 oz can crab meat, drained
400g/14 oz can creamed corn
¾ cup heavy cream
2 egg yolks
12 oysters
2 tablespoons fresh chopped basil
salt and freshly ground black pepper

1 Heat wine in a large saucepan over medium heat. Add garlic and simmer for 2–3 minutes.
2 Add fish stock, oregano, green onions, crab, corn and half the cream. Bring to a boil, reduce heat to low. Cover and simmer for 5 minutes.
3 Combine remaining cream with egg yolks. Gently stir cream and eggs into soup. Do not allow soup to boil.
4 Remove from heat stir through oysters and basil and season with salt and pepper.

Serves 4 • Preparation 20 minutes • Cooking 15 minutes

Creamy Mussel Soup

1kg/2 lb fresh mussels
500g/1 lb shrimp with shells on
1 large onion, chopped
2 stalks celery, chopped
2 large carrots, chopped
¼ cup parsley, chopped
8 cups fish stock
2 cups white wine
3 shallots, chopped
1¼ cups heavy cream
salt and freshly ground black pepper

1 Scrub and remove beards from mussels. Soak in clean water for at least 3 hours before use. Peel shrimp, place the heads and shells into a boiling pot. Reserve the peeled shrimp for another meal or deep freeze for another occasion.

2 Add the onion, celery, carrot, parsley, fish stock and white wine to the pot. Bring to a boil and then simmer for 45 minutes. Strain and reserve stock.

3 Place the mussels in a suitable size pot, pour in the stock and add the shallots. Boil for 20 minutes. If you need more liquid, add some white wine. Before serving, add the cream and check seasoning. Serve with fresh crusty bread.

Serves 6 • Preparation 1 hour • Cooking 1 hour 10 minutes

Mussels with Wine and Tomatoes

1½kg/3 lb mussels
400g/14 oz fresh tomatoes, halved
⅓ cup olive oil
4 cloves garlic, crushed
1 brown onion, chopped
½ cup white wine
400g/14 oz canned peeled tomatoes
¼ cup tomato paste
½ cup fish stock
10 sprigs fresh oregano, leaves removed and chopped
salt and freshly ground black pepper

1 Preheat the oven to 180°C. Wash mussels under water, scrub the shells with a
   scourer, and remove their beards. Discard any mussels that are open.
2 Place halved fresh tomatoes on a baking sheet, drizzle with olive oil, sprinkle with
   salt and roast in the oven for 20 minutes.
3 Heat a little oil in a saucepan and sauté the garlic and the onion until soft. Add the
   white wine and cook for 2 minutes. Add the roasted tomatoes, canned tomatoes,
   tomato paste, stock and chopped oregano. Simmer for 5–10 minutes. Season with
   salt and pepper. Add mussels, cover, and cook for an additional 5 minutes, until
   mussels have opened. Discard any that do not open.
4 Serve with crusty bread.

Serves 6 • Preparation 1 hour • Cooking 40 minutes

Shrimp and Pasta Soup

1½kg/3 lb cooked shrimp
1 small onion, chopped
1 stalk celery, chopped
1 small carrot, chopped
300g/10 oz cooked pasta
2 tablespoons olive oil
4 large cloves garlic, chopped
4 sprigs fresh oregano, leaves removed and chopped
1 large sprig basil, chopped
400g/14 oz canned chopped tomatoes
2 tablespoons tomato paste
1 teaspoon salt
1 teaspoon freshly ground black pepper
½ cup dry vermouth

1 Peel the shrimp, place the heads and shells into a boiling pot, add the onion, celery and carrot. Cover with 6 cups water and boil for 20 minutes, then strain. Reserve the stock and make sure you push all the juice from the heads with the back of a wooden spoon. Discard the solids.

2 Bring a large saucepan of salted water to a boil, add the pasta and cook for 8 minutes or until just firm in the center (al dente). Drain, set aside and keep warm.

3 In a saucepan, heat the oil, add all remaining ingredients except the shrimp and cook for 5 minutes. Add the stock and boil for an additional 15 minutes. Reduce the heat, add the shrimp and cook for 3 minutes.

4 Reheat the pasta by pan frying or running under hot water. Divide between six soup bowls and ladle the soup into the bowls. Serve with crusty bread.

Serves 6 • Preparation 40 minutes • Cooking 1 hour

Seafood Bisque

90g/6 tablespoons butter
1 small onion, diced
1 clove garlic, crushed
1 small carrot, diced
1 stalk celery, sliced
3 cups fish stock
2 tablespoons lemon juice
1 bay leaf
1 sprig thyme, leaves removed and stalks discarded
¼ teaspoon Tabasco sauce
½ teaspoon Worcestershire sauce
1 cup heavy cream
1kg/2 lb seafood (shrimp, scallops, fresh fish filets), finely diced
½ cup dry white wine
1 lemon, thinly sliced
¼ cup parsley, chopped

1 Melt butter and sauté onion and garlic for 5 minutes. Add carrot and celery and cook
   for an additional 3 minutes.
2 Combine the fish stock, lemon juice, bay leaf, thyme, Tabasco and Worcestershire
   sauce, add to the pot and simmer for 30 minutes or until vegetables are tender.
   Remove bay leaf. Puree the mixture, add cream, seafood, wine, and reheat, but do not
   let boil. Garnish with lemon and parsley.

Serves 8 • Preparation 40 minutes • Cooking 45 minutes

Spicy Thai Soup

1 tablespoon vegetable oil
550g/1 lb raw shrimp, shells removed and reserved
2 small red chilies, seeded and cut into long thin strips
1 tablespoon paprika
¼ teaspoon ground red pepper
1½ quarts/liters chicken stock
¾ in/2cm strip lemon zest
¾ in/2cm strip lime zest
1 can straw mushrooms, drained
juice of 1 lemon
juice of ½ lime
2 tablespoons light soy sauce
fresh cilantro, to garnish

1 Heat wok over medium-high heat for 2 minutes. Add oil to wok: it should start to smoke. Carefully add shrimp and 1 red chilli and stir-fry for 1 minute.

2 Add paprika and ground red pepper. Stir-fry for 1 minute longer. Remove shrimp mixture and set aside.

3 Add shrimp shells to wok and stir-fry for 2 minutes until shells turn orange. Add chicken stock and lemon and lime zest and bring to a boil. Cover, reduce heat and simmer for 15 minutes. Strain the soup and return the liquid to the saucepan.

4 Add mushrooms and shrimp mixture to the soup and bring to a simmer. Stir in the lemon and lime juice, soy sauce and remaining red chilli. Garnish with fresh cilantro.

Serves 4 • Preparation 10 minutes • Cooking 25 minutes

Lobster Bisque

1 small cooked lobster
1 large carrot, diced
1 small onion, finely chopped
125g/4½ oz butter
¾ cup dry white wine
1 bouquet garni
6 cups fish stock
½ cup rice
salt and freshly ground black pepper
⅛ teaspoon cayenne pepper
½ cup heavy cream
2 tablespoons brandy
¼ cup parsley, chopped

1 Cut lobster in half lengthwise, remove flesh from shell and set aside. Wrap shell in an old kitchen towel, crush with a hammer and set aside. Cook carrot and onion in half the butter until softened but without coloring, about 5 minutes. Add crushed shell, cook for an additional minute, then add wine. Boil until reduced by half. Add bouquet garni, stock and rice and cook.

2 After about 20 minutes, when rice is tender, remove large pieces of shell and bouquet garni. In small batches, purée in a food processor with remainder of the butter. Pour through a strainer. Rinse out food processor to remove every trace of shell and purée strained liquid again, this time with lobster flesh, saving a few pieces for garnish. Reheat gently.

3 Add salt, pepper and cayenne pepper, then stir in cream, brandy and reserved lobster pieces, cut into thin slices. Serve very hot and garnish with parsley.

Serves 4 • Preparation 30 minutes • Cooking 45 minutes

Vegetable

Tempt your palate with aromas of fresh tomatoes and bell peppers, garlic and herbs. Add freshly grated cheese and warm bread for a delicious experience like no other. Or try our French Onion soup for a taste sensation, where the garlic just waits to add extra flavor to a beautiful traditional soup.

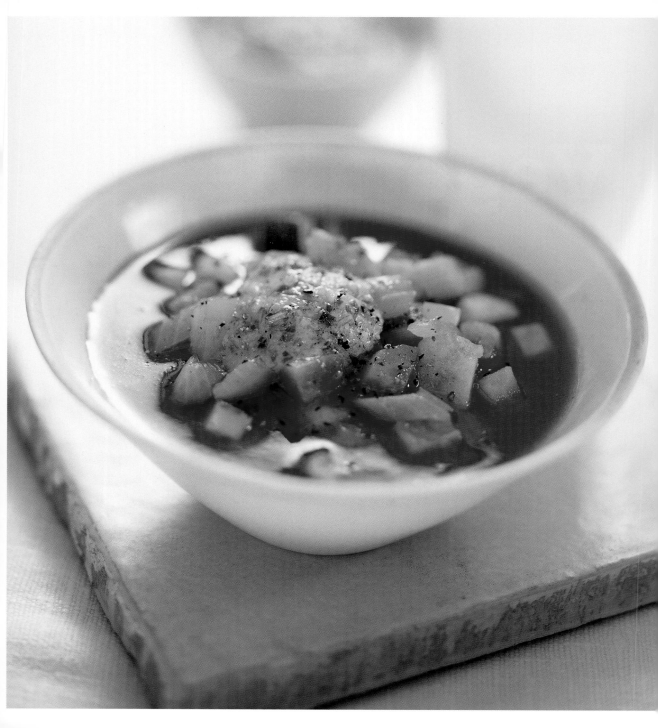

Provençal-Style Soup

2 tablespoons extra virgin olive oil
1 onion, chopped
1 medium potato, peeled and chopped
1 carrot, chopped
1 yellow bell pepper, deseeded and chopped
500mL/17 oz vegetable stock
2 stalks celery, chopped
2 zucchini, chopped
400g/14 oz canned chopped tomatoes
1 tablespoon tomato purée
sea salt and freshly ground black pepper

Green onion Pesto
6 green onions, roughly chopped
50g/1.8 oz Parmesan, grated
4 tablespoons extra virgin olive oil

1 For the soup, heat the oil in a large heavy-based saucepan, then add the onion,
   potato, carrot and yellow bell pepper. Cook uncovered for 5 minutes over a
   medium heat, stirring occasionally, until the vegetables just start to brown.

2 Add the stock, celery and zucchini and bring to a boil. Cover and simmer for
   10 minutes or until the vegetables are tender. Stir in the tomatoes, tomato purée
   and season generously. Simmer uncovered for 10 minutes.

3 Meanwhile, make the pesto. Place the green onions, Parmesan and oil in a food
   processor and process together to a fairly smooth paste. Ladle the soup into
   bowls and top with a spoonful of the pesto.

Serves 4–6 • Preparation 20 minutes • Cooking 25 minutes

Borscht

4 medium beets
4 cups chicken stock
1 onion, peeled and studded with 4 cloves
1 bouquet garni*
1 tablespoon sugar
1 tablespoon lemon juice
salt
¼ cup sour cream

1 Peel and slice 3 of the beets. Cook in the stock with onion and bouquet garni until quite tender. Cook the remaining beet, without peeling, in boiling water until tender. Allow to cool, peel and grate or cut into julienne strips.

2 Remove herbs and onion and purée cooked beet. Add sugar, lemon juice, salt and the grated beet to the purée. Chill thoroughly. Garnish with a spoonful of sour cream and serve.

Serves 8 • Preparation 3 hours • Cooking 45 minutes

Cheddar Cheese Soup

60g/4 tablespoons butter
3 medium onions, finely diced
3 tablespoons all-purpose flour
salt and freshly ground black pepper
½ teaspoon paprika
¼ teaspoon sage
pinch of cayenne pepper
3 cups milk
1 cup heavy cream
160g Cheddar cheese, grated
½ teaspoon Worcestershire sauce
3 drops Tabasco sauce
⅓ cup whipped cream
½ small bunch chives, chopped

1 Melt butter in a saucepan over a medium heat, add onions and sauté until tender. Add flour, spices and seasonings and cook for 3 minutes.
2 Gradually add milk and cream and cook, stirring continuously over a low heat until thick and smooth. Add cheese and stir until melted. Season with Worcestershire sauce and Tabasco.
3 Garnish with cream, sprinkle with chives and serve.

Serves 6 • Preparation 15 minutes • Cooking 20 minutes

Cauliflower Soup

750g/1½ lb cauliflower florets
200g/7 oz onions, chopped
6 cups chicken stock
6 cups milk
2 teaspoons salt
¼ teaspoon cayenne pepper
½ cup heavy cream
¼ cup parsley, chopped

1 Combine the cauliflower, onions, stock and milk in a large boiling pot. Cook until the cauliflower is broken down. Remove from heat.
2 Blend the cauliflower and liquid, then return to the pot.
3 Season with salt and cayenne pepper, then add the cream. Reheat and serve garnished with chopped parsley.

Serves 8 • Preparation 30 minutes • Cooking 40 minutes

Cream of Vegetable Soup

60g/4 tablespoons butter
750g/1½ lb prepared vegetables (see below)
2 cups chicken stock
salt and freshly ground black pepper
½ cup heavy cream
¼ cup parsley, chopped

Pumpkin and Leek
500g/1 lb pumpkin, peeled and chopped
2 leeks, thinly sliced
¼ cup dry sherry

1 Melt the butter in a saucepan, add vegetables and cook for 10 minutes over medium heat.
2 Add stock and seasonings and simmer over low heat until vegetables are tender. Purée mixture.
3 Stir in cream and reheat without boiling. Garnish with parsley and serve immediately.

Variations:
Carrot (750g/1½ lb carrots, peeled and roughly chopped; ½ teaspoon allspice); Broccoli (750g/1½ lb broccoli, divided into florets; ½ teaspoon nutmeg); Zucchini (750g/1½ lb zucchini, sliced; ¼ teaspoon basil); Asparagus (750g/1½ lb asparagus, ends broken off, stems cut in half); Mushroom (750g/1½ lb mushrooms, washed and sliced; ½ teaspoon oregano; garnish with thinly sliced mushrooms); Celery (750g/1½ lb celery, chopped; 1 teaspoon curry powder)

Serves 6 • Preparation 30 minutes • Cooking 45 minutes

Chunky Tomato Soup

750g/1½ lb ripe tomatoes, chopped
1 potato, peeled and chopped
1 small onion, chopped
1 sprig fresh basil
1 teaspoon sugar
2 tablespoons tomato paste
salt and freshly ground black pepper
1 cup vegetable stock
¼ cup heavy cream
¼ cup parsley, finely chopped

1 Place all ingredients except parsley and cream into a saucepan with the stock.
   Bring to a boil and simmer, covered, for 20 minutes.
2 Serve soup with a swirl of cream and sprinkle with chopped parsley.

Serves 4 • Preparation 20 minutes • Cooking 30 minutes

Cream of Asparagus with Basil

1kg/2 lb fresh asparagus
2 tablespoons butter
4 large shallots, finely chopped
20 basil leaves
6 tablespoons flour
pinch of saffron threads

6 cups chicken or vegetable stock
salt and freshly ground pepper to taste
2 egg yolks
1 cup whole milk or half and half
peanut oil for frying
large basil leaves, extra

1 Cut the tips off the asparagus and drop in boiling water for 30 seconds. Drain and set aside. Cut the remaining stalks into ¾ in/2cm lengths. Melt the butter and sauté the asparagus stalks for two minutes. Add the shallots and basil leaves and continue cooking for 5 minutes or until the vegetables have softened.

2 Sprinkle the flour over the vegetable mixture and stir thoroughly, making sure that all the flour is mixed in. Add the saffron and chicken or vegetable stock and bring the mixture to a boil, stirring often.

3 Simmer for 20 minutes or until the vegetables are tender. Puree the soup with a blender or food processor. Return to saucepan and season with salt and pepper.

4 Whisk the egg yolks and milk together. Slowly add to the puréed soup, whisking constantly. Cook over low heat for five minutes, until hot.

5 To prepare the fried basil leaves, heat a little peanut oil then add a few basil leaves at a time (take care as leaves will splatter for a few seconds). Remove the leaves as soon as they stop sizzling and drain on paper towel. Repeat with remaining basil leaves. Garnish with the reserved asparagus tips, fried basil leaves, and a drizzle of cream.

This rich soup, with a subtle flavor of saffron and basil is delicious hot or at room temperature.

Serves 6–8 • Preparation 30 minutes • Cooking 40 minutes

Vegetable Soup with Pesto

500g/18 oz cannellini beans, rinsed and drained
1 large onion
500g/18 oz green beans
500g/18 oz zucchini
5 medium potatoes
30g/2 tablespoons butter
2–3 slices bacon, chopped
8–10 cups water
2 teaspoons salt

Tomato Basil Paste
1 cup basil leaves, finely shredded
4 cloves garlic, crushed
2 ripe tomatoes, peeled and chopped
1 tablespoon tomato paste
½ cup romano cheese, grated
3 tablespoons olive oil

1 Chop the onion finely. Trim the green beans and cut into short lengths. Cut zucchini into thick slices. Peel the potatoes and dice.

2 Melt butter in a large pan and sauté bacon and prepared vegetables until softened, about 5 minutes. Add cannellini beans and salt; cover with cold water, cover and simmer gently for 1 hour.

3 Combine basil leaves and garlic in a food processor. Add tomatoes, tomato paste and cheese. Puree. Gradually pour in olive oil and puree until smooth. Stir into the soup just before serving.

Tomato Basil Paste

1 Combine basil leaves and garlic in a bowl. Add the tomatoes to the basil with tomato paste and cheese. Pound this mixture in a blender or food processor to make a smooth paste. Gradually beat in olive oil. Set aside to serve with soup.

Serves 4–6 • Preparation 10 minutes plus soaking • Cooking 1 hour 30 minutes

Cream of Spinach Soup

500g/18 oz spinach or swiss chard, trimmed
10–12 fresh sorrel leaves
45g/3 tablespoons butter
1 small onion, finely chopped
340g/12 oz potatoes, peeled and sliced
5 cups chicken stock
salt and freshly ground black pepper, to taste
freshly grated nutmeg, to taste
2 tablespoons fresh parsley, chopped
1 egg yolk
1 cup heavy cream
extra heavy cream and fresh chives

1 Wash and dry the spinach and sorrel on paper towels, roughly chop them, then blend in food processor until pureed.

2 Heat the butter in a saucepan, add the onion and cook over a moderate heat, stirring, until soft. Add the potatoes and stir until the potatoes are well coated with butter. Add the stock and bring to a boil.

3 Lower the heat and simmer, partially covered, for 15 minutes or until the potatoes are tender. Remove from the heat, season to taste with salt, black pepper and nutmeg and cool slightly.

4 Purée the mixture with ground greens and parsley, in batches, in a blender or food processor. Return to a clean saucepan and bring to a simmer.

5 Mix the egg yolk with the cream in a bowl, stir in a little of the hot soup, then return the mixture to the saucepan. Heat through without boiling. Serve in heated bowls with a swirl of extra cream and a few chives.

Serves 6 • Preparation 10 minutes • Cooking 30 minutes

Sorrel Soup

50g/3½ tablespoons butter
1 medium sized onion, finely diced
1 stalk celery, thinly sliced
1 leek, white part only, thinly sliced
1 small carrot, washed and diced
1 tablespoon finely chopped parsley
salt and pepper
1kg/2 lb fresh sorrel
1½ quarts/liters good beef or chicken stock
sour cream for serving

1 Heat butter in a frying pan, add onions and gently fry until transparent, stirring occasionally. Add the prepared celery, leek, carrot and parsley and cook while stirring for 4 minutes. Season with salt and pepper; set aside.

2 Trim off the thicker lower part of the stem of the sorrel and wash well. With water still clinging to leaves, place in a large saucepan. Pour in 1 cup boiling water, cover and boil slowly for 6 – 8 minutes. Cool slightly then puree in a blender or food processor with the liquid.

3 Pour the stock into the large saucepan, add the fried vegetables, cover, and simmer for 20 minutes. Adjust seasoning.

4 Serve with sour cream.

Serves 6–8 • Preparation 20 minutes • Cooking 35 minutes

Roasted Tomato, Red Pepper and Bread Soup

1kg/2 lb plum tomatoes
2 red peppers
3 tablespoons extra-virgin olive oil
3 cloves garlic, crushed
2 onions, finely chopped
2 teaspoons ground cumin
1 teaspoon turmeric
1 teaspoon ground cilantro
4 cups vegetable or chicken stock
2 slices whole-wheat bread, crusts removed and torn into pieces
1 tablespoon balsamic vinegar
salt and pepper

1 Preheat the oven to 425°F/220°C.
2 Place the tomatoes and peppers in a lightly oiled baking dish and bake for
   20 minutes or until the skins have blistered. Set aside to cool, then remove the
   skins and roughly chop.
3 Heat the oil in a saucepan, add the garlic and onion and cook for 5 minutes,
   or until soft. Add the cumin, turmeric and cilantro, and cook for 1 minute until
   well combined. Add tomatoes, peppers and bouillon to the saucepan, bring to
   a boil and simmer for 30 minutes. Add bread, balsamic vinegar and salt and
   pepper, and cook for an additional 5–10 minutes.
4 Serve with fresh cilantro and Parmesan cheese, if desired.

Serves 4 • Preparation 10 minutes • Cooking 1 hour

Butternut Squash Soup

1 tablespoon olive oil
1 onion, finely chopped
2 cloves garlic, crushed
1 long red chilli, deseeded and finely chopped
5 cups vegetable or chicken stock
1kg butternut pumpkin, peeled and diced
2 tomatoes, roughly chopped
½ cup cream
2 tablespoons freshly chopped cilantro
1 tablespoons freshly chopped mint
salt and freshly ground black pepper
¼ cup grated Parmesan cheese

1 Heat oil in a large saucepan over medium heat. Cook onion, garlic and chilies until soft.

2 Add stock, pumpkin and tomatoes. Bring to a boil, reduce heat to low. Cover and simmer for 20 minutes or until pumpkin is tender.

3 Puree soup until smooth. Return soup to the heat. Stir through cream, cilantro and mint. Season with salt and pepper.

4 Serve soup with grated parmesan cheese.

Serves 4–6 • Preparation 20 minutes • Cooking 30 minutes

Spicy Sweet Potato Soup

1 tablespoon olive oil
1 leek, halved, washed and sliced
3 cloves garlic, freshly crushed
1½ tablespoons Thai seasoning
750g/1½ lb sweet potatoes, peeled and roughly chopped
750g/1½ lb carrots, peeled and roughly chopped
5 cups chicken stock
400mL/14 oz coconut milk or light coconut milk
salt and freshly ground black pepper

1 Heat the oil in a large saucepan. Over medium heat add the leek and garlic and cook
   until soft. Add the Thai seasoning and cook until aromatic.
2 Add the sweet potatoes, carrots, stock and coconut milk. Bring to a boil. Cover and
   simmer for 30 minutes or until the vegetables are soft.
3 Purée the soup in a blender until smooth. Return the soup to the saucepan and cook
   until heated. Season to taste. Spoon into bowls and drizzle with extra coconut milk.
   Serve with crusty bread.

**Cut off and discard the root and green leaves from the leek. Cut the white part of the
leek in half lengthways. Remove the outer layer and wash the leaves to remove the dirt.**

Serves 4–6 • Preparation 15 minutes • Cooking 33 minutes

Mushroom Barley Soup

4 tablespoons butter or oil
1 large onion, finely diced
2 quarts/liters beef stock
1 medium carrot, peeled and diced
1 large potato, peeled and diced
½ cup pearl barley
1 bay leaf
1 tablespoon chopped fresh dill or ½ teaspoon dried
500g/18 oz button or field mushrooms
1½ tablespoons lemon juice
thin cut lemon slices for garnish

1 Heat half the butter or oil in a large saucepan, add the onion and gently fry
  until soft. Stir in the stock and bring to a boil. Add the carrot, potato, barley,
  bay leaf and dill. Simmer for 1 hour, stirring occasionally.

2 Wipe over the mushrooms with damp paper, trim the stem end and slice
  mushroom thinly.

3 In a large pan heat remaining butter or oil and fry the mushrooms gently for
  3–5 minutes tossing frequently. Add to the simmering soup and simmer for
  15–20 minutes more. Taste and adjust seasoning and stir in the lemon juice.

4 Serve in soup bowls garnished with lemon slices and sprig of dill floating
  on surface.

Serves 6–8 • Preparation 25 minutes • Cooking 1 hour 30 minutes

Pumpkin Soup

1½kg/3 lb pumpkin, peeled and cut into large cubes
2 tomatoes, chopped
1 large onion, chopped
5 cups vegetable stock
pinch of salt
pinch of cayenne pepper
⅔ cup heavy cream
¼ cup parsley, finely chopped

1 Combine pumpkin, tomato and onions with the stock in a pan. Simmer gently until pumpkin is tender, approximately 20 minutes.

2 Purée pumpkin mixture. Return to pan, add salt, cayenne pepper and cream and reheat gently.

3 Serve sprinkled with parsley.

Pumpkin soup is also delicious chilled

Serves 6 • Preparation 20 minutes • Cooking 30 minutes

Minestrone

⅓ cup olive oil
1 medium onion, sliced
1 clove garlic, crushed
250g/½ lb potatoes, peeled and chopped
150g/5 oz carrots, thinly sliced
125g/4½ oz celery, thinly sliced
150g/5 oz zucchini, sliced
4 cups vegetable stock
400g/14 oz canned diced tomatoes
rind from piece of Parmesan cheese
¼ cup parsley, chopped
400g/14 oz canned cannellini beans
salt and freshly ground black pepper

1 Heat the oil in a saucepan and cook the onion and garlic for 5 minutes until onion is tender. Add the potatoes and cook for an additional 5 minutes. Repeat with the carrots, celery and zucchini.

2 Add the beef stock, tomatoes and cheese rind, bring to a boil and simmer covered for 1 hour. If the soup becomes too thick, add more stock.

3 Add the chopped parsley and cannellini beans, and heat for an additional 10 minutes.

4 To serve, remove the cheese rind, season with salt and black pepper, and serve with crusty bread.

Serves 6 • Preparation 20 minutes • Cooking 1 hour 30 minutes

Celery Leek Soup

90g/6 tablespoons butter
½ head celery, chopped
1 leek, sliced
2 carrots, peeled and chopped
2 egg yolks
20g/4 tablespoons Parmesan cheese, grated
1 cup heavy cream
¼ cup parsley, chopped

1 In a large saucepan, melt butter over a low heat. Add vegetables and, stirring occasionally, cook gently until leek is transparent. Add 2 cups water, cover and simmer gently until vegetables are tender. Purée.
2 Combine the egg yolks, Parmesan and cream. Gradually stir egg mixture into soup and heat gently over a low heat without boiling. Garnish with parsley and serve.

Serves 8 • Preparation 30 minutes • Cooking 30 minutes

Potato Watercress Soup

1 medium bunch watercress, coarsely chopped
1kg/2 lb potatoes, peeled and roughly chopped
4 cups milk
1¼ cups vegetable stock
salt and freshly ground black pepper
chopped fennel leaves

1 Simmer the potatoes in the milk and stock. Add the watercress when the potatoes are nearly cooked, then cook for an additional 10 minutes.

2 Purée the ingredients in a blender or food processor. Season with salt and pepper, and chill completely. Serve with the chopped fennel or dill leaves. Garnish with croutons and sour cream.

Serves 4 • Preparation 25 minutes • Cooking 50 minutes

Corn and Red Pepper Chowder

1 sprig fresh cilantro
30g/2 tablespoons butter
400g/14 oz canned corn
2 red bell peppers, diced
1 small onion, finely chopped
1 small red chili, finely chopped
1 tablespoon all-purpose flour
2 cups vegetable stock
½ cup heavy cream

1 Trim the leaves off the fresh cilantro and finely chop the root and stems.
2 Heat the butter in a large saucepan over medium heat. Add the corn kernels, bell pepper, onion and chilli and stir to coat the vegetables in the butter. Cook, covered, over low heat, stirring occasionally, for 10 minutes, or until the vegetables are soft.
3 Increase the heat to medium and add the cilantro root and stem. Cook, stirring, for 30 seconds, or until fragrant. Sprinkle with the flour and stir for an additional minute.
4 Remove from the heat and gradually add the vegetable stock, stirring together.
5 Add 2 cups water and return to the heat. Bring to a boil, reduce the heat to low and simmer, covered, for 30 minutes, or until the vegetables are tender. Cool slightly.
6 Ladle about 2 cups of the soup into a blender and purée until smooth. Return the purée to the soup in the saucepan, pour in the cream and gently heat until warmed through. Season to taste with salt. Sprinkle with the cilantro leaves to serve.

Serves 2 • Preparation 35 minutes • Cooking 1 hour

Fruit

Normally one would expect to see fruit made into juice or salad, however in this chapter we have selected some great fruit soups, both hot and cold. We offer a range of great tastes of fruit – try the Cantaloupe Soup or the Sour Lemon Soup, you will be pleased with the results.

Almond Soup

200g/7 oz almonds
1 clove garlic, peeled
¼ cup parsley, finely chopped
8 slices stale bread, preferably wheat bread
⅓ cup olive oil
1 teaspoon ground cumin
½ teaspoon saffron
4 cups chicken stock
1 cup milk
salt and freshly ground black pepper

1 Fry almonds, garlic, parsley and 4 slices of bread in about 4 tablespoons of oil.
   When golden, put the contents of the pan in a food processor and puree with
   cumin, saffron and a little stock. Put in a saucepan, pour in remaining stock and
   milk, season with salt and pepper and bring to a boil. Lower the heat and cook
   slowly for about 15 minutes.

2 Fry remaining bread slices in remaining olive oil until crisp and golden.

3 Bring the soup to a boil again and add 4 slices of fried bread. Cover, remove from
   the stove and leave for 5 minutes before serving.

Serves 4 • Preparation 15 minutes • Cooking 40 minutes

Cantaloupe Soup

1 large cantaloupe, halved and seeds removed
4 tablespoons/60g butter
2 teaspoons sugar
grated zest of 1 lemon
pinch of salt
3 cups milk
sprigs of mint

1 Using a melon baller, scoop out 12 balls of melon and reserve. Coarsely chop the remaining flesh.
2 Heat the butter over a low heat, add the coarsely chopped melon, sugar, lemon zest and salt and simmer for 4 minutes. Add milk and bring to a boil.
3 Purée mixture and chill. Garnish with reserved melon balls and mint sprigs.

Serves 4 • Preparation 15 minutes plus 2–3 hours chilling • Cooking 15 minutes

Sour Lemon Soup

7 cups chicken stock
2 stalks lemongrass, bruised
4 small fresh lemon leaves
2 tablespoons fish sauce
250g/9 oz mushrooms, thinly sliced
3 tiny fresh chilies, washed and bruised
500g/18 oz lobster meat or raw shrimp or chicken, chopped
juice of 1 lemon
¼ cup fresh cilantro leaves

1   Combine stock, lemongrass, lemon leaves, fish sauce, mushrooms and chilies.
    Bring to a boil, add seafood or chicken and simmer for 3–4 minutes.
2   Add lemon juice to taste. Remove the lemongrass, sprinkle with cilantro leaves
    and serve immediately.

Serves 8 • Preparation 30 minutes • Cooking 15 minutes

Pineapple Soup

1 medium pineapple, cored, peeled and chopped
2 small cucumbers, peeled, seeded and chopped
1 cup pineapple juice
1 cup apple juice
juice of 1 lemon
1 red bell pepper, finely diced
1 yellow bell pepper, finely diced
2 small red chilies
1 medium red onion, finely sliced
¼ cup fresh dill, chopped
¼ cup flat-leaf parsley, chopped, plus 6 whole sprigs
salt and freshly ground black pepper
1 tablespoon olive oil
1 teaspoon Tabasco sauce

1 Place the peeled and chopped pineapple, chopped cucumbers, pineapple juice, apple juice, lemon juice, half the red and yellow bell pepper, the chilies, onion, dill and parsley in a blender or food processor and process until almost smooth.

2 Transfer the mixture to a bowl and season to taste with salt and pepper then chill until ready to serve.

3 Heat a little oil then fry the parsley sprigs until bright green and brittle. Drain on paper towel.

4 Ladle the soup into bowls and sprinkle with remaining yellow and red bell pepper and deep-fried parsley sprigs. Drip the Tabasco sauce into the soup, around the garnish, and serve.

Serves 6–8 • Preparation 20 minutes plus 2 hours chilling • Cooking 5 minutes

Tomato Leek Soup

400g/14 oz white leek, washed and finely chopped
6 cups chicken stock
600g/20 oz tomatoes, peeled, seeded and chopped
1 teaspoon salt
½ teaspoon lemon pepper
1 sprig basil, chopped

1 Place the finely chopped leeks into a boiling pot and cover with the chicken stock.
   Bring to a boil. Cook for an additional 5 minutes and then add the tomato. Boil until
   the tomato is cooked. Remove from the heat and add the salt, lemon pepper and
   basil. Serve with a spoonful of sour cream and a sprig of basil.

Serves 6 • Preparation 30 minutes • Cooking 45 minutes

Pumpkin, Parsnip and Pear Soup

1½kg/3 lb pumpkin
1 tablespoon olive oil
500g/18 oz parsnip, peeled and diced
2 small brown pears, peeled and diced
1 large red onion, chopped
3 cloves garlic, minced
1 tablespoon curry powder
salt and freshly ground black pepper
6–8 cups vegetable stock
½ cup dry white wine
½ cup plain yogurt
1 bunch chives, chopped

1 Preheat the oven to 375°F/190°C. Cut the pumpkin in half and place in a baking sheet with ½ cup of water and bake for about 90 minutes or until the pumpkin is tender. Scoop out and discard the seeds and peel away the skin.

2 Heat the olive oil in a large saucepan and add the diced parsnip, diced pears, chopped onion, garlic, curry powder and salt and pepper to taste and sauté, stirring occasionally, for about 20 minutes. Add the cooked pumpkin, stock and white wine and bring to a boil. Simmer uncovered for about 40 minutes then purée the soup until smooth.

3 To serve, drizzle some yogurt over the soup and scatter the chives on top.

Serves 6–8 • Preparation 30 minutes • Cooking 2 hours 30 minutes

Avocado Soup with Dill and Smoked Trout

3 ripe avocados
juice of 1 lime
4 green onions
3 tablespoons plain yogurt
3 tablespoons sour cream
4 cups vegetable stock
1 teaspoon Tabasco sauce
2 teaspoons Worcestershire sauce
150g/5 oz smoked trout
¼ cup fresh dill, chopped
salt and freshly ground black pepper

1 Peel the avocados and remove the stones. Reserve 1 avocado, dice the flesh and then drizzle with a little of the lime juice to keep it green.

2 Place the remaining avocado flesh and green onions in a blender or food processor and blend with the remaining lime juice, yogurt, sour cream, stock, Tabasco sauce and Worcestershire sauce until the mixture is smooth. Add 3½ oz/100g smoked trout and half the dill and process for one extra second. Season to taste with salt and pepper.

3 Gently warm the soup through until just warm then serve garnished with the remaining flaked trout, avocado and dill.

Serves 4 • Preparation 30 minutes • Cooking 10 minutes

Roasted Vegetable Soup

2 tablespoons extra virgin olive oil
1 large sweet onion, chopped
2 carrots, peeled and diced
2 stalks celery, chopped
2 cloves garlic, minced
½ in/1cm piece fresh ginger, finely chopped
3 teaspoons fennel seeds, dry-fried for 2 minutes then crushed
½ fennel bulb, chopped
1 teaspoon sea salt
800g/28 oz canned crushed tomatoes
3 cups vegetable stock
freshly ground black pepper
¼ cup fresh cilantro, chopped

1 Heat oil in heavy saucepan. Add onion and sauté on medium heat until translucent.
2 Add carrots, celery, garlic, fresh ginger, crushed fennel seeds, fresh fennel bulb and sea salt. Simmer until soft, approximately 5–10 minutes.
3 Add tomatoes, stir and cook briefly. Add vegetable stock. Bring to a boil, stirring constantly. Cover and simmer for 20 minutes.
4 Place small amounts in a blender or food processor and blend until smooth. Return to saucepan. Add fresh ground pepper, and cilantro. Stir and serve, garnished with chopped fennel leaves.

Serves 4 • Preparation 10 minutes • Cooking 30 minutes

Cold

How about a delightful iced soup to cool the palate on a very hot and stressful day? Or just sit around the pool, or relax with a good book, and you will find that an iced soup is just the ticket to get the taste buds going. Try our Gazpacho with just a hint of chili or a creamy Vichyssoise just to soothe the nerves.

Cold Beetroot Soup

500g/18 oz fresh beets
1½ quarts/liters water
2 teaspoons salt
1½ teaspoons sugar
⅔ cup sour cream
2 medium sized cucumbers, peeled and sliced
4 green onions, thinly sliced
4 radishes, thinly sliced
2 tablespoons finely chopped fresh dill
2 tablespoons lemon juice
salt and freshly ground black pepper to taste
3–4 hard boiled eggs, chopped

1 Peel and coarsely grate the beets, wearing rubber gloves. Place beets in a stainless steel saucepan, add the water and bring to a boil. Reduce heat to moderate and cook uncovered for 10 minutes.

2 Reduce heat to low, stir in the vinegar, salt and sugar, simmer partly covered for 25 minutes. Drain the beets through a sieve over a bowl to retain the liquid. Cool beets and liquid separately to room temperature.

3 Beat the sour cream into the cooled beet liquid. Stir in the beets, cucumber, green onions, radishes, dill and lemon juice. Season to taste with salt and pepper. Cover and refrigerate 2 hours or longer until thoroughly chilled.

4 Garnish with chopped egg.

Serves 6 • Preparation 25 minutes plus 2 hours chilling • Cooking 35 minutes

Red Pepper Fennel Soup

2 tablespoons olive oil
2 leeks, white part only, chopped
1 onion, chopped
2 cloves garlic, chopped
2 shallots, chopped
5 large carrots, chopped
2 fennel bulbs, halved, cored and chopped
4 sprigs fresh thyme
2–3 red bell peppers
1 cup white wine
4½ cups chicken or vegetable stock
salt and freshly ground pepper
3 tablespoons plain yogurt

Corn Mint Salsa

2 ears of corn
½ small onion, finely diced
1 Roma or plum tomato, seeded
10 fresh mint leaves, finely sliced
2 sprigs fresh cilantro, chopped
⅓ cup chopped fresh parsley
juice of 1 lime
salt and freshly ground pepper

1   Heat the olive oil in a saucepan and add the leeks, onion, garlic and shallots and
    sweat for 5 minutes until soft. Add the carrots, fennel and thyme sprigs and cook
    over a medium heat for 30 minutes until all the vegetables are tender.

2   Grill the red peppers until blackened and blistered. Transfer to a plastic bag and
    allow to steam for a few minutes. When cool enough to handle, remove the skins
    and slice the peppers into strips.

3   Add peppers, wine and stock to the softened vegetables, and cook, uncovered on
    high heat for about 20 minutes. Remove from heat and puree in a food processor
    or blender. Season to taste with salt and pepper and chill for 1 hour.

4   Make salsa by cutting the corn off the ears and microwaving for 2 minutes. Stir in
    the onion, tomato, herbs and lime juice. Season to taste.

Serves 8 • Preparation 25 minutes plus 1 hour chilling • Cooking 1 hour 5 minutes

Chilled Asparagus Soup

300g/10 oz fresh asparagus
4 cups chicken stock
40g/3 tablespoons butter
40g all-purpose flour
2 cups heated milk
½ cup heavy cream
15g/1 tablespoon Parmesan cheese

1 Trim tough ends from asparagus. Place in a saucepan and cover with chicken stock. Bring to a boil and cook for 10 minutes.

2 Remove the asparagus and chop off and reserve some of the tips for garnish. Purée the asparagus and strain. Reserve the strained pulp. Reduce the chicken stock to a quarter by boiling at high heat.

3 In a separate saucepan, melt the butter and add the flour. Combine and remove from the heat after 2 minutes. Add milk, stirring constantly.

4 Add the reduced chicken stock and asparagus pulp. Stir and return to the heat. Stir frequently for 10 minutes.

5 Add the cream and Parmesan. Season with salt and pepper and refrigerate until chilled. Garnish with reserved asparagus tips.

Serves 6 • Preparation 30 minutes plus 2–3 hours chilling • Cooking 30 minutes

Chilled Yogurt Soup

1 large cucumber
1 cup heavy cream
200mL/6½ oz natural yogurt
2 tablespoons white wine vinegar
1 tablespoon balsamic vinegar
¼ cup fresh mint, chopped
1 clove garlic, crushed
salt and freshly ground black pepper

1 Peel and grate the cucumber.
2 Combine the cream, yogurt and vinegars, and whisk, until smooth. Stir in the cucumber, mint, garlic and seasoning. Cover and chill for three hours.
3 Stir and taste for seasoning before serving. Garnish with a slice of cucumber, a sprig of mint and cracked pepper.

Serves 4–6 • Preparation 15 minutes plus 3 hours chilling • Cooking 3 hours

Gazpacho

2 slices of stale bread
2kg/4 lb tomatoes, roughly chopped
1 cucumber, peeled and chopped
1 green bell pepper, seeded and chopped
1 small onion, chopped
2 cloves garlic, chopped
5 tablespoons olive oil
1–2 tablespoons wine vinegar
1 teaspoon cumin seeds or ground cumin

1 Soak bread in a little water, and squeeze it out before using (the bread helps to thicken the soup and give it a nice consistency).
2 Blend all vegetables and garlic in a blender or food processor, and push through a strainer into a bowl. Use the blender again to mix bread, oil and vinegar together. Add some of the tomatoes, the cumin seeds and salt to taste. Add a little water and mix into the bowl with the soup. Add a few ice cubes and let sit until chilled, adding more water if necessary.

Serves 6–8 • Preparation 15 minutes plus 2 hours chilling

Chilled Dill Soup

2 cups vegetable stock
1 large onion, chopped
4 zucchini, chopped
1 large potato, chopped
½ teaspoon ground cumin
1 cup sour cream
2 tablespoons chopped fresh dill
sprigs fresh dill

1　Place stock, onion, zucchini, potato and cumin in a large saucepan and bring to a boil. Reduce heat and simmer for 20 minutes or until potatoes are tender. Remove saucepan from heat and set aside to cool slightly.
2　Place soup mixture in a food processor or blender and process until smooth. Transfer soup to a large bowl, stir in sour cream and dill, then cover and chill for 3 hours before serving. Ladle soup into chilled bowls and garnish with dill sprigs.

Serves 4 • Preparation 20 minutes • Cooking 25 minutes

Iced Tomato Soup

3 slices bread, crusts removed
1kg/2 lb tomatoes, peeled, seeded and chopped
1 cucumber, peeled, deseeded and chopped
½ onion, chopped
2 cloves garlic, crushed
½ green bell pepper, deseeded and chopped
1 teaspoon salt
1 teaspoon ground cumin
2 tablespoons olive oil
2 tablespoons wine vinegar

Garnish
1 red or green bell pepper, diced
1 small cucumber, diced
1 onion, finely chopped
2 hard-boiled eggs, chopped
croutons

1 Place all ingredients in a large bowl and allow to stand for 30 minutes to soften bread and blend flavors.
2 Purée one-third of the mixture at a time in a blender or food processor. Pour back into a bowl and thin down to desired consistency with 2–3 cups iced water.
3 Cover and chill. Adjust seasoning to taste. Serve in chilled bowls or in a large bowl over ice.
4 Garnish with assorted toppings.

Serves 8 • Preparation 20 minutes plus 2 hours chilling

Cold Squash Soup

500g/18 oz peeled, seeded butternut squash
250g/9 oz leek, chopped and washed
8 cups chicken stock
1 teaspoon salt
¼ teaspoon cayenne pepper
½ teaspoon paprika
½ cup heavy cream
¼ small bunch chives, chopped

1 Place squash, leek, and stock in a boiling pot and place over a high heat. Boil until the squash has broken down.
2 Remove from the heat and add the salt, cayenne pepper and paprika. Blend or process to a very fine consistency, check seasoning.
3 Chill for 2–3 hours before service.
4 To serve, add cream and garnish with chopped chives.

Serves 6 • Preparation 25 minutes plus 2–3 hours chilling • Cooking 1 hour

Cool Cumin-Yogurt Soup

1 teaspoon cumin seeds
1 teaspoon black cumin seeds
1 tablespoon butter
4 green onions, finely sliced
10 fresh mint leaves
2 teaspoons ground cumin
1 teaspoon turmeric
60g/¼ cup cashews
300g/10 oz can chickpeas, drained and
rinsed

500g/18 oz plain lowfat yogurt
200mL/8 oz sour cream
200mL/8 oz water
salt and pepper to taste
600g/1⅓ lb cucumbers
1 tablespoon sugar
2 tablespoons shredded coconut, toasted
mint leaves, for garnish

1 Heat a dry skillet. Add cumin seeds and toss until toasted, about 3 minutes. Remove from the pan and set aside.

2 Add the butter to the pan and add green onions and mint leaves and sauté for a few minutes until wilted. Add the cumin, turmeric and cashews and toss until the spices are fragrant and the nuts are golden. Add the drained chickpeas and cook for an additional 2 minutes. Set aside.

3 In a mixing bowl, whisk together the yogurt, sour cream and water until smooth. Season to taste with salt and pepper. Peel the cucumbers and scrape out the seeds. Cut the cucumber flesh into thin slices and add to the yogurt mixture. Chill for 1 hour before serving.

4 Add the green onion/spice mixture and sugar to the yogurt and stir thoroughly to combine.

5 Garnish with toasted coconut, sliced mint leaves and cumin seeds.

Serves 6 • Preparation 30 minutes • Cooking 1 hour 15 minutes

Vichyssoise

60g/4 tablespoons butter
2 leeks, washed and thinly sliced
1 medium onion, thinly sliced
500g/18 oz potatoes, peeled and sliced
3 cups chicken stock
salt and freshly ground black pepper
¾ cup heavy cream
¼ small bunch chives, chopped

1 Melt butter in a saucepan, add leeks and onion and sauté until tender without browning. Add potatoes, stock and seasonings and simmer until soft. Purée.
2 Chill for 2–3 hours. Adjust seasonings, stir in the cream and serve in chilled bowls garnished with chopped chives.

Serves 4 • Preparation 20 minutes plus 2–3 hours chilling • Cooking 40 minutes

Index